D0049637

This book belongs to

Romance

NORMAN ROCKWELL

ARIEL BOOKS

ANDREWS AND McMEEL

KANSAS CITY

ISBN: 0–8362–4709–4

Frontispiece: THE DIARY
Saturday Evening Post cover, June 17, 1933

Book design by Susan Hood

Romance

SERENADE

Saturday Evening Post cover
September 22, 1928

MARRIAGE LICENSE

Saturday Evening Post cover
June 11, 1955

KNOWLEDGE IS POWER

Saturday Evening Post cover
October 27, 1917

LATE NIGHT OUT

—

Saturday Evening Post cover
March 9, 1935

UNREQUITED LOVE

Saturday Evening Post cover
October 2, 1926

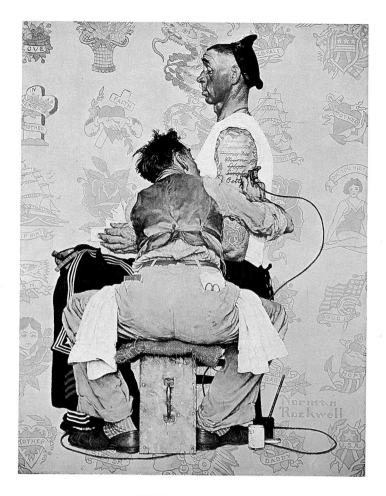

THE TATOOIST

—

Saturday Evening Post cover
March 4, 1944

DREAMBOATS

Saturday Evening Post cover
February 19, 1938

MIDNIGHT ROMANCE

Saturday Evening Post cover
March 22, 1919

THE CORSAGE

———

Saturday Evening Post cover
May 25, 1957

THE OUIJA BOARD

Saturday Evening Post cover
May 1, 1920

CHOOSE ME

Saturday Evening Post cover
May 4, 1929

CAVE OF THE WINDS

Saturday Evening Post cover
August 28, 1920

YOUNG LOVE

———

Saturday Evening Post cover
July 11, 1936

LOOKING AT LOVE

Saturday Evening Post cover
August 12, 1944

THE BREAKFAST TABLE

Saturday Evening Post cover
August 23, 1930

THE WINDOW WASHER

Saturday Evening Post cover
September 17, 1960

THE PALM READER

Saturday Evening Post cover
March 12, 1921

PARIS

Saturday Evening Post cover
January 30, 1932

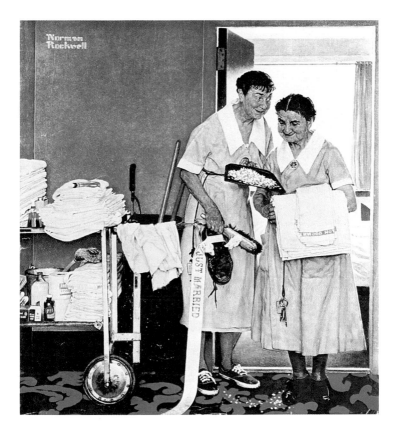

BRIDAL SUITE

Saturday Evening Post cover
June 29, 1957

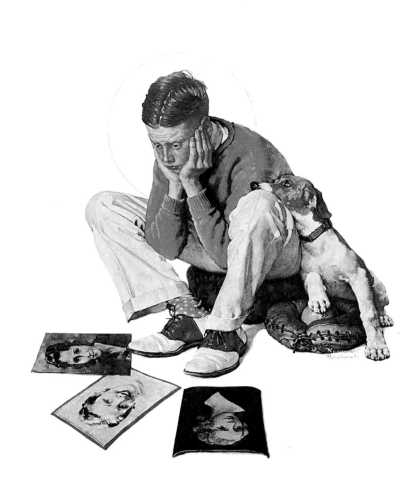

STARSTRUCK

—

Saturday Evening Post cover
September 22, 1934

GETTING READY

Saturday Evening Post cover
September 24, 1949

ACCORDION PLAYER

———

Saturday Evening Post cover
August 30, 1924

PARK BENCH

Saturday Evening Post cover
November 21, 1936

THE ARTIST

Saturday Evening Post cover
June 4, 1927

LETTERMAN

—

Saturday Evening Post cover
November 19, 1938

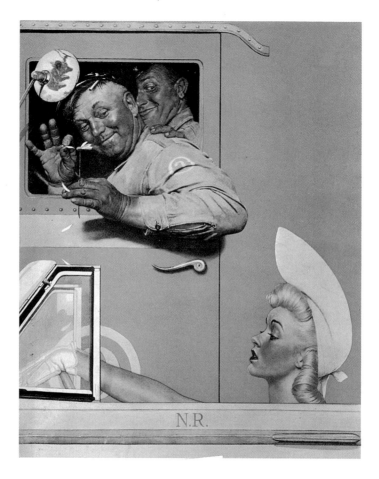

LOVES ME...

Saturday Evening Post cover
July 26, 1941

GO HOME!

—

Saturday Evening Post cover
June 19, 1920

THE OLD COUPLE

Literary Digest cover
April 15, 1922

UNIVERSITY CLUB

———

Saturday Evening Post cover
August 27, 1960

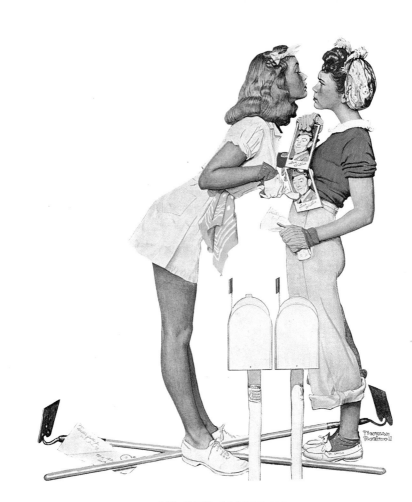

AT THE MAILBOX

Saturday Evening Post cover
September 5, 1942

SUNSET

Saturday Evening Post cover
April 24, 1926

THE RIVALS

—

Saturday Evening Post cover
September 9, 1922

PRIVATE LIFE

Saturday Evening Post cover
March 21, 1942